"Dream big, work hard, and never be afraid to turn your imagination into reality."

-Natcole Staskiewicz

I am capable of achieving great things.

My potential is limitless, and I am constantly growing.

I believe in my ability to overcome challenges.

I am a valuable and unique individual.

I am in control of my own happiness.

I am surrounded by supportive and caring people.

I am worthy of success and happiness.

I have the power to make a positive impact on the world.

I am resilient and can bounce back from setbacks.

I am constantly learning and improving.

I am a problem solver, and I can find solutions to any challenge.

I am confident in my ability to face difficulties.

I am kind, compassionate, and make a difference in the lives of others.

I embrace change and see it as an opportunity for growth.

I am a leader, and I inspire others with my actions.

I am patient and trust that everything will work out for the best.

I am proud of the progress I've made so far.

I have the courage to express my true self.

I am responsible for my own choices and actions.

I am open-minded and always willing to learn from others.

I choose to focus on the positive aspects of my life.

I am surrounded by love, and I love and appreciate myself.

I am deserving of success and happiness.

I believe in my ability to achieve my goals.

I am a good friend, and my friendships are important to me.

I am grateful for the opportunities life gives me.

I am proud of who I am becoming.

I am surrounded by abundance, and I attract success.

I have the power to create positive change in my life.

I am responsible for my own happiness, and I choose to be happy.

I am confident and capable in everything I do.

I am a positive influence on those around me.

I am resilient, and I can handle whatever comes my way.

I am a magnet for success, and I attract positive outcomes.

I am a valuable member of my community.

I am constantly evolving and growing into the best version of myself.

I am a source of inspiration for others.

I am confident in my ability to achieve my goals.

I am surrounded by people who believe in me.

I am patient and trust that everything unfolds in perfect timing.

I am capable of learning from my mistakes and growing stronger.

I am a problem solver, and I can find solutions to any challenge.

I am in control of my thoughts and choose to think positively.

I am loved.

I am confident in my unique style and fashion.

I am a good listener, and I respect the opinions of others.

I am enough.

I am open to new experiences and opportunities.

I am a beacon of light and positivity.

I am a unique and special person, and I celebrate my individuality.

I am kind to myself and others.

I am worthy of love and respect.

I am constantly learning and growing.

I am a source of positivity and joy.

Your inner superpower is the unwavering belief in your limitless potential.

I am capable of handling whatever comes my way.

I am beautiful or handsome.

I am grateful for my health and well-being.

I am in perfect harmony with the universe.

I am a force to be reckoned with, unwavering in my determination.

I am an empowered creator of my own destiny.

I am unapologetically authentic.

I am grateful for the lessons life teaches me.

"Every mistake is a chance to learn and grow. Embrace challenges, for they make you stronger."

I let go of self-criticism and embrace self-love, just as my inner child would.

"Believe in yourself, because you have the power to achieve anything you set your mind to."

"Your uniqueness is your superpower. Celebrate what makes you different, and let it shine."

Kindness is a strength. Be the reason someone smiles today.

The world is full of possibilities. Explore, be curious, and never stop discovering the wonders around you.

Your thoughts and ideas are like seeds — plant them, nurture them, and watch them grow.

Success is not about being perfect; it's about perseverance and learning from every experience.

The more you practice gratitude, the more reasons you'll find to be grateful.

Don't be afraid to ask questions; curiosity is the key to unlocking knowledge.

In a world where you can be anything, be kind.

Every step you take is a step toward a brighter future. Keep moving forward.

Your words have power. Speak kindly to yourself and others.

You are a masterpiece in progress — embrace the journey of becoming your best self.

Challenges are opportunities in disguise. Face them with courage and determination.

Mistakes are proof that you are trying. Keep trying, keep learning, and keep growing.

I cherish the memories of my happy and carefree moments from childhood.

Your smile is a gift to the world. Share it generously.

Success is not measured by what you have but by who you are and how you treat others.

You are not alone. Reach out when you need help, and offer a helping hand to others.

Be a rainbow in someone else's cloud. Spread joy wherever you go.

Your potential is limitless. Don't underestimate the incredible person you are becoming.

The more you read, the more things you'll know. The more that you learn, the more places you'll go.

Your actions speak louder than words. Choose them wisely.

Life is a journey, not a destination. Enjoy the ride and savor every moment.

You are a star in your own story. Shine bright and light up the world.

The more you give, the more you receive. Generosity is a gift to both the giver and the receiver.

Listen to your heart; it knows the way to your truest dreams.

Let your imagination play.

You are not defined by your past. Every day is a new opportunity to rewrite your story.

You are a work of art, and there is beauty in your uniqueness.

Your actions today shape the person you become tomorrow. Make each moment count.

Setbacks are setups for comebacks. Rise stronger every time you face a challenge.

You are a problem solver. Approach challenges with creativity and determination.

Your future is a blank canvas. Paint it with the colors of your dreams and aspirations.

www.KinderPress.org

Made in the USA
Columbia, SC
08 November 2024